Red Clay & Vinegar

To David English
My special friend
and respected colleague

RED CLAY & VINEGAR

*Looking at Family
Through the Eyes
of a Southern Child*

NAOMI HAINES GRIFFITH

Red Clay & Vinegar
P.O. Box 68275
Nashville, TN 37206
redclaynhg@aol.com

ISBN 1-57966-021-5

Design by Randell Williams
Printed in the United States of America
5 4 3 2 1

To

EULA M. HAINES

Contents

A Dedication Story

SEVERAL years ago my mother asked me to take her back home to Iuka, Mississippi, out to the Mt. Evergreen community, to see where she went to school. We drove out from Iuka and stood in the middle of the road and looked at the place where the school had been. She proudly told me her daddy had helped build the school when the children out that way had no place to go.

As she shared her memories with me, she explained that the school's one room had benches. The front bench was first grade. Each time a student was promoted, he moved back one row, until he reached the last row and was in seventh grade. After that a child had to go into Iuka to school, which meant that the family had to pay room and board during the week. Mother said her family couldn't afford that expense so she had to stop at the seventh grade.

Knowing how special she is, I said, "Mother, I wish you could have gone on. You're so smart, and it would have meant so much to you."

She stood quietly for a minute and softly said, "I would have liked to have gone on, but I would have liked to have gone for you."

Because I am so proud of her, the way she has lived her life, cared for her children, and left memories more precious than a raft of college degrees, I have dedicated this book to my mother, Eula M. Haines.

Preface

WHEN it's our own life, and it is so close and familiar, most of us never pick up the *good* parts, the ones that are smooth and satisfying, and ask ourselves, "Why did it happen this way?" It just never occurred to me to take a look at how I knew what to do as a mother, why I knew to always be there for my children, to put them to bed with a quiet time together, to talk about right and wrong, to listen. However, the day came in 1971 when I had to answer those questions.

When I picked up the phone at the office that day, I heard the warm, familiar voice of the woman doctor at the health department. She was calling early and her tone was serious and worried. Like so many calls I received then, this one immediately brought a feeling of responsibility and then a sense of helplessness.

Skipping the usual Southern social questions about my children and the weather, Dr. Morris said, "We had a baby in well-baby clinic today that is losing weight. It's the second time in a row. This one's probably a 'failure to thrive' and you know what that means. The mom is fifteen, and you need to do something quick."

Hearing the urgency and concern in those words, I also understood the expectation that was both spoken and implied. My job was to save the situation, save a baby, make the girl a mother, work a miracle.

I drove west from Decatur, Alabama, over our county line, turning off the main road onto a winding gravel road that dissolved into packed dirt and mud. The road wound back into Morgan County. It grew smaller and smaller, running between fence rows and property lines. I parked the car at the end of the road, and gathered my plastic legal notebook that seemed always to identify me as the "welfare lady." I felt better when I held this legal pad inside my left arm and next to my breast, as a shield from the hurt and sometimes from danger.

From my car I had a long walk, first in the last remaining ruts in the end of the muddy road and soon in a tall stand of weeds and grass, always aiming toward a lonesome trailer in the middle of the field. It was old and rusty, just sitting where some old truck had pulled it roughly into place and dropped it.

After I walked across the big field to the edge of a cleared spot, I stopped and reached down to pick beggar lice from my skirt and stockings. There were nicks in my hose from the weeds and mud rimmed my shoes. Standing there with the fall wind blowing unhindered across the field, I felt as alone and unprotected as the trailer house.

I looked to see if there was a telephone line leading to the trailer. There was none. There was no car around, either.

Since there were no steps up to the metal door, I grabbed the door handle, hung on, and reached up and knocked with my other hand. It opened quickly, yet slowly, and I was very close to the knees of a fifteen-year-old girl. When I looked up into her eyes, she seemed scared and wary.

I said, "I'm Naomi Griffith from the Department of Pensions and Security, and I'm here to check on your baby."

Without a word, she stepped back. I almost threw myself up into the trailer. After I got used to the near darkness inside, I saw the baby lying to my right on an old horsehair sofa, sucking a bottle propped up on a ragged towel. The girl still didn't say anything, but I sat down in a split vinyl trailer chair, looked into her eyes, and explained the call from the health department. She just looked at me.

Feeling so uncomfortable, and wanting to get right to it, I said, "Tell me how you take care of your baby, Judy." In the back of my mind I knew not to call clients by their first names, but I just couldn't say *Mrs.*

She didn't look at me, but quickly said, "See, I feed her." I gently told her that was good, and asked her what else she did.

"I change her. Look at those diapers." There was a stack under the window, and I told her that was really good. Then I nudged her on, asking what else she did for the baby.

She said, "I give her a bath. She's clean. Just look."

I made no attempt to get up, but again said that was good. Finally, I said, "What else do you do for her?" There was no answer.

After a minute of silence, I asked her quietly, "Judy, do you hold the baby close to you? Do you talk to her or sing her a song? Do you let her feel your heart beat through your clothes and the warmth of your body? Does she know your smell?"

With a sudden look of almost sadness, she replied, "Oh, my mama told me that if I picked her up much or held her, I'd spoil her, so I don't lessin I have to."

I sat silently, not knowing where to start. She didn't really touch her baby, and I had a hollow, empty feeling inside myself that was overwhelming. How would I explain that sense in me at that very moment that reached out in love to my baby at home, the baby I loved to hold, to kiss, to hear breathe?

Knowing I had to do something right then to help Judy and her baby, I drove back to the office. I got a copy of an old Dr. Spock child care book that was lying in the cluttered catch-all we called the library. As I drove back to the trailer, it hit me that Judy could not read well enough to use the book. I knew from the case record that after years of sporadic attendance she had dropped out of school the year before.

For a second time, I went over the muddy road and the weeds, threw myself up into the trailer, sat back in the plastic chair, and began to read to her. I'd read a page, and we'd talk about it. Then I'd read another page, and we'd talk about it. She seemed interested.

I went to Judy's two or three times a week for the next few weeks. Finally, after six or eight visits, I was reading the section on "When Your Baby Is Sick." Judy suddenly jumped up, stood in the middle of the floor in front of me, and—almost in pain—shouted, "How dare you say I'm not a good mother?"

I quietly said, "Judy, I didn't say that."

"Yes, you did too!"

"No, I didn't mean to."

In hurt and frustration, Judy yelled, "Lady, how would I know how to be a good mother when I've never seen one?"

She was right. My heart broke for her and her baby. I was

asking her to do something that she had never seen, never experienced. She never had a mother who put her first, and she knew it.

As I was driving back to Decatur, Judy's pain led me to begin looking carefully at the *good* parts of my life to see where I came from, where I learned to love myself and my babies, where my life was really made. I started by remembering that when my first baby was born at Ft. Bragg, North Carolina, my mother at age sixty-seven, rode the Greyhound bus for eighteen hours to show me how to take care of her.

The following stories represent a long journey over many years. As I have picked up and looked at my memories, I have found answers in stories of just living day to day, going to school and taking my family with me, standing by my mother and learning about death, and feeling joy in the celebration of life and family. These memories, captured in stories, are word pictures of the feelings I brought with me from childhood.

Remember, these stories are seen and and told through the eyes of a little Southern girl forty to fifty years ago. Children remember feelings more than facts, and feelings are truth to me.

Red Clay & Vinegar

Iuka

MY family is from a little north Mississippi town called Iuka. I think it was named for an Indian chief. Many of the place names around there reflect the heritage of the Choctaw, Cherokee, and Creek nations. Iuka is also known for a group of seven springs all bubbling up within one block. The block is called "Spring Park," and my mother and daddy were married at its southeastern gate in 1922.

Iuka's other claim to fame is that for years it was the "Marrying Capital of the South." Couples ran off to Iuka to get married because there was no waiting period, no cooling-off time, no blood test, and the license only cost one dollar. If a boy and girl were out on a date and, in a fit of passion, the boy said, "Let's run off and get married," that meant Iuka, Mississippi. Actually, people would just say "They ran off to Iuka," and we all understood. The old justice of the peace who performed most of the marriages was called Brother Gober; before he died sometime back they said he had married eighteen thousand couples.

We moved back to Iuka at least twice during the early years of my life. One of these times, we lived in Miss Bama's house. I was big enough then to go to town on Saturday by myself or with a friend. We would go down to the Tishomingo County courthouse square, and our favorite thing was to watch all of the people go in and get married. They went in, some of them barefoot, some in overalls, some in long wedding dresses and evening gowns, every kind of way you can think of. We would all sit outside, and they would come out in a minute or two married and, if they had it, we would all throw the rice. We'd be part of the wedding party.

The other thing we did on Saturday mornings says a lot about old Southern ways. There was an old man who would show up there on Saturday morning and sit on a bench in the courthouse square. He would wear Liberty overalls, the ones that have that little green triangle piece up on the bib.

He was grizzled and gnarled, but he was very special because he could *rub off warts*. People up North and other places are too sophisticated to believe this could really happen, but he could do it. He had what some called a "healing gift" or "the power." People would come by and pay him a nickel to rub off their warts. I realize now that his art was a part of the old ways of the South, the folk medicine of my people. He rubbed one off for me. Now it didn't fall off right that minute. It took a couple of weeks, but it went away.

As a child in Iuka, my Saturday mornings were pretty much made up of weddings and warts. I loved it.

⁓

When I decided to work for myself, I wanted a name for my company that reflected my background, my attitude toward life, and my pride in my family. The name Red Clay and Vinegar leapt into my mind. I thought about it in the context of my past and my roots and it fit perfectly.

The red clay of north Alabama and north Mississippi is the heart of cotton farming. The clay is so red that when it is wet it doesn't look like dirt, but like it's been fired in an oven. It's the kind of red clay that grows cotton and is peculiar to the really deep South. Folks used it to make poultices along with tar, sulphur, and anything else they had, hoping to cure the ills of their children since calling the doctor was almost unheard of. The red clay is also where my people are laid to rest. At all funerals there was a big pile of it near the grave, waiting to seal away the life of someone I knew. We also played in it, and slid down banks of it. The red clay—almost impossible to wash out—was always on children's backsides. The red clay that would not wash out has stayed in my heart all these years.

When I think of vinegar, it brings back the smell of making kraut in a churn, making pickles all summer, and watching mother cut fresh cucumbers into a dish and cover them with vinegar. It also helps with cleaning, eases the sting from insect bites, and takes the frizz from curly hair. Vinegar, like love in a family, takes up a lot of slack and makes most things better.

For me, Red Clay and Vinegar just says it all.

Snowdown

FIVE miles out from Iuka on a gravel road is a little community called Snowdown. It's interesting to say out from Iuka because Iuka is *out,* but Snowdown is *further out.* Growing up, when we drove to Snowdown, we'd go past the houses of people we knew—the Mosers, the Bullards, the Wingos, people that Mother knew who lived out that way. As the years passed, one by one they were gone.

Five miles out there in the middle of that community is Snowdown United Methodist Church. Back then it was just Snowdown Methodist Church. It's a little red brick church sitting in a grove of big oak trees with a circle around the church and the cemetery.

In little grave plots in that cemetery behind the church, six generations of my people—back to the early eighteen hundreds—are buried in the red clay of north Mississippi.

The most important day of the year in my childhood was the first Sunday in July. It was called Homecoming and later on just "Snowdown." It was and is our all-day singing, dinner on the grounds, decoration day for all the people there in the Snowdown community. Everybody who could make the trip came home for that Sunday. It was a great celebration of family and roots, remembering who we are, seeing each other, and renewing old times. A very, very special day.

Snowdown is always the hottest day of the year. It's what I call a trickle-down day, when the sweat just trickles down your whole body no matter what you have on. In the early years, there was no air conditioning. We'd get out there under the trees and try to stay cool. We'd go inside to sing in the afternoon, and, oh, it would be so hot, even with people fanning away with the fans from Cutshall Funeral Home.

I can remember so well those first Sundays in July when I was a little girl of four, five, and six years old. Early in the morning I would start to wake up to clinking noises in the kitchen where Mother was cooking. I'd wake up with the smell of chicken frying on the edges of my dreams. She would be frying a chicken or two to take to Snowdown, frying them with lard in a big black iron skillet. She would have killed those chickens and dressed them the day before.

I also knew that she would be cooking green beans. We had a big garden and she'd pick the green beans and snap them and have them ready to cook early that morning to be fresh to go down to Snowdown. They were cooked the old-time way in a big iron pot with a big piece of fatback.

You know, what we have done to green beans in this country in recent years ought to be a Class A felony. We've allowed the yuppies to take our green beans and try to make them healthy. They hold them under hot water for a few seconds and serve them. I've told my children that if you put a green bean in your mouth and it crunches, spit it out, it's not fit to eat. I see them sometimes served on plates at banquets and luncheons and there will be three or four whole green beans lying there, not even snapped and just as green as they can be—or, as my mother would say, they don't even have the greenie out.

She would have cooked hers in that big iron pot down real low with that fatback until there was only a drop of two of water in the bottom of the pot, and they would almost fry around in the bottom. They'd be dark and so good. There's just no other way to cook those green beans but Mother's way. She'd make potato salad, without any grating or adding anything fancy like olives or celery. It was potatoes and boiled eggs, pickles that she cut up, mayonnaise, and onion. It was wonderful.

Next she would pack our lunch to go to Snowdown. This was a long time before the days of picnic baskets. She would put our lunch in a big, white enamel dishpan with a red ring around the outside and cover it with a luncheon cloth.

A little later, Mother would come into the room where I was sleeping and say, "Come on, Naomi."

We would go out in the yard together. It would still be early enough that the dew would be on the grass, and she would have a five-gallon water bucket and a pair of scissors. She would always have zinnias around the garden to keep the bugs away. We'd fill the water bucket with zinnias and daisies and gladiola out of our yard to take to Snowdown, to decorate the graves of our people.

We'd pack the bucket with flowers in the car along with the lunch and start out down to Snowdown. I'd be so excited I could hardly stand it.

In those early years, Daddy would be driving, with Mother sitting in the front seat, and Shirley and me in the back seat. We couldn't wait to get down there. It was a wonderful day. It was thirty-five miles down there but it took about an hour in those days. We would pull up in the yard of the church, usually about ten-thirty or eleven o'clock in the morning.

My job was to go with my mother out to the cemetery. She'd get the bucket of flowers, along with fruit jars that she'd gathered up from canning. We'd go out through the gate to the cemetery and start at the first grave of our people. My job was to get a stick or a rock or something to dig a little hole in the top of the grave in that hard July-baked red clay.

I would dig a little hole, she would hand me the fruit jar, and I'd place it down in that hole. Then, as she handed me the flowers to go in the fruit jar, I'd say "Mama, who's this?"

She'd say, "Oh, Naomi, that's your PawPaw Sanders. Your PawPaw Sanders was a Dutchman. He was wide as he was tall. We used to think that if he fell over, he'd roll all the way to Eastport." (That's the place we all used to go swimming out on the lake.)

She said, "He loved to eat. He loved every part of the hog from the tail to the ears. He loved chitlins, he loved crackling bread, he liked brains and eggs, he liked everything about that hog, and he loved things cooked in lard. He lived to be eighty-nine years old, never saw a doctor in his life, and died when he got a briar in his ear that set up blood poisoning."

"You know, Naomi," she said, "if I remember right, the day he died was in the early spring and he set out cabbage plants that day. He was too old to bend over so he would dig the hole with the end of his walking cane and drop the cabbage set in the hole and cover it up with his foot. That's your PawPaw Sanders."

Then we would go to the next grave. I'd dig the hole, and

put in the fruit jar. She'd hand me the flowers and I'd say, "Who's this?"

With the same feeling each year, she'd say "Oh, that's your Aunt Anne. Your Aunt Anne was a beautiful woman. She loved pretty things and Will liked to buy them for her. She died when she was thirty-five years old and it broke his heart. He was really never the same again. That's your Aunt Anne."

We'd go to the next grave and put the flowers in the jar, and I'd say, "Who's this?"

With pride in her voice she'd say, "Oh that's your Uncle Billy. Your Uncle Billy helped to build this church. He was the superintendent of Sunday School here for twenty-five years. People out here really respected and thought a lot of him. That's your Uncle Billy."

We'd go down those graves one at a time and talk about each one. There'd be hurt, there'd be joy, there'd be pride, there'd be disappointment, but we talked about every one. As we talked about them, I'd get this feeling inside of me, this warm feeling, and I was filled up with the sense of it all, of being part of something like that, of being part of a family.

When we'd get to the end of those graves, stand up, and gather up the rest of the jars and the pieces of flowers, I would stand there and look at those graves and I felt so tall. I felt so full of myself, of being connected, of knowing who I was and where

I came from. I'd stand there and have this tremendous sense of peace and pride in my heart.

In that long row of graves, there were really good people. There were some that maybe could have been better. Now by the world's standards, not a single person there was important or significant. There was not a high school graduate, much less a college graduate. There was no one who had owned a company, been a CEO of anything, been written up in any magazine, or received any award. There was nothing special about those people except that they were my people, and that's where I came from and that's who I am.

When we came out of the cemetery, it was time to think about spreading our lunch. When we came through the gate, Mother would have to hold me back by grabbing the sash of my dress. I was ready to go. I wanted to be everywhere. I was going to see everybody. I knew there'd be chewing gum and Coca-Cola, and it was going to be a big day.

She'd say, "Wait a minute, Naomi. I've got two things I want to tell you." She told me the same two things for years. "First of all, there's no running water out here. If you get thirsty, the only water is over there in that vat on the back of that pickup truck."

She said, "On the side is a dipper on a string. Don't put your mouth on that dipper. You know, people out here dip snuff, chew tobacco, no telling what they've had, colds, the flu. I don't want you drinking after people."

The second thing that she'd tell me is a woman thing. It's just something that women say to their children.

She'd say "Now, Naomi, when we spread our lunch under those trees down there, you don't eat anybody's food until you talk to me about it. No telling about these people. Some of them are good housekeepers, some aren't. Some of them don't put their food up after meals and it's had flies on it. I don't want you eating after everybody. Now, you can have Doad Thorne's chicken and dumplings, and you can have Verdie Mae's apple and orange cake, but other than that, you gotta come talk to me about it."

Now these warnings were necessary for me because I am what's called a menopause baby, a baby born to a mother over forty. Another term for us that's more socially acceptable is "born late." When you're a menopause baby and you get here and you're okay, it's just like a gift to the world, to the whole family.

As a result, there were really no rules for me. Part of it was that Mother was too old to keep up with me, but the other part was that she was at a point of her life where all the little nitpicky things just didn't matter anymore. She just loved me and waited on me to catch hold. Still, she felt like she had to tell me those things, knowing all the time that it wouldn't make any difference.

I'd go over to that pickup truck and I'd look up at the dipper and think, "Well, there's no problem. I'll just put my mouth around here by the handle where nobody else has put theirs. There won't be a problem here."

I'd get me a big drink of water. Of course, probably everybody else out there was doing the same thing. It didn't matter.

Then I'd look over at the women spreading the food on those long tables under the trees. This was so exciting to a little old country girl. I'd get my plate that Mother had in the dishpan or in a sack and start down those tables. I'd get one of everything I wanted: chess pies, egg custard stacked up, fried pies, chicken and dressing, deviled eggs. It was just so grand. She knew I'd do it. I guess we both knew I would. But her telling me and reminding me were part of the ritual of growing up special.

Snowdown is a memory at the very heart of my understanding of family. It's the place where I found out who I was over and over again. It was a celebration of family and a way of life that made families first, before friends, before work, before money. Family was the most important thing I could feel.

~

After many years of forgetting, we are coming back to the idea that family traditions and rituals are basic to building a sense of family pride. Family pride is essential to building healthy families, for it can, and usually does, focus on family uniqueness, strengths, love, and responsibility. I love it when a little child says, "At our house we celebrate Christmas by _____."

Of course, every family is different, with its own history, memories, stories, and songs. That makes it special. Each child should be able to "wallow" in the uniqueness of his or her family, talk about family, and feel the fabric of past generations.

For my Brother and me
We would not open up presents
on christmas until mom
Had made coffee AND
Both mom & Dad Had
Had at Least one cup
or more.

The Day We Found Uncle Hiram

[handwritten: July 2 1889]

[handwritten: the First walk on the moon]

MOTHER was born January 1, 1900 so her life covers a century and many important events. She has seen two world wars, the Great Depression, the New Deal, the Korean War, and the Vietnam conflict. She has buried a husband, her only son, and a daughter. She sees things in a broad way, and she has a perspective that I can only imagine.

Because of this perspective, she often neglects to mention little things that I would find interesting. I guess they just don't seem important to her. My daughter Amy now tells me that I don't know how to make small talk, so I may be moving in the same direction.

It was only two years ago that Mother dropped the name of Nettie, the woman who delivered me at home. Nettie lived nearby and stepped in when the doctor was late arriving. How big a deal is it anyway that a ten-pound baby was being born to a forty-one-year-old mother out in the country?

Until I was an adult with my own children, I thought that all my relatives were buried at Snowdown. Then, one day when Mother asked me to take her out to Mt. Evergreen to look for the place her one-room school had stood, we got into a discussion about her family. She mentioned that she had a great-uncle at Campground Cemetery.

The next year, my son Wade was working on a genealogy merit badge in Boy Scouts. We worked on family trees for days, ending up at Snowdown Cemetery walking around with Mother and my sister Lois. Wade must have asked her a thousand questions about family. He was especially interested, as I had been thirty-five years earlier, in the gravestone with the picture of the somber soldier in a plastic-covered frame on the front.

Again Mother brought up Campground and her missing relative as if he was lost only yesterday. In a directory of Tishomingo County cemeteries that she borrowed from her cousin, she had seen his name listed at Campground, and we decided to find him.

With directions from a cousin who carried the mail, we drove down several gravel roads until we saw a beautiful white church in a grove of oak trees. It had been a place the Confederate troops had camped, and, therefore, was given its historic name. The cemetery started behind the church and went up a slight hill to the woods.

Wade raced ahead of us up the hill, looking quickly at each grave, searching for something that said Sanders. Before I could get to the first grave, Wade shouted, "I've found him! I've found Hiram!"

There in the first row of graves, one of the earliest graves there, was Hiram Sanders. He did not have a gravestone as such, but someone had taken a pasteboard box, poured concrete in it, let it set up, tore the box away before the concrete was too hard, and scratched:

Hiram Sanders

Died 1830

As we stood there Mother commented, "He died over here in the winter, and there was no way to get him to Snowdown." The distance was five miles.

After that Wade talked about Hiram as if he knew him. We now had located the oldest grave in our family, and it was like a homecoming to all of us. Uncle Hiram was a real person again.

~

My time in the cemetery has been a celebration and a remembrance. My children seemed to feel the same way as they walked among the graves, read the epitaphs, subtracted dates to get ages, and talked about family. I have loved to watch my son run among the tombstones looking for the grave of the eighteen-year-old soldier, whose marker carries a picture of a happy boy with a cocked military hat caught forever in time.

There is no doubt that this process of dealing with death crystallizes our sense of who we really are and how we fit into the fabric of family.

Bill Haines

AT the funeral of my aunt last year in Iuka, I talked with an old friend of my family who lives in the Snowdown community and really knows who we are. My daughter was standing there, and I introduced her to this good-natured seventy-year-old man.

I said, "Amy, this is Diddler Thorn."

He stuck out his hand and said, "My mother called me Diddler when I was a little boy and it stuck. My real name's Edward."

Caught up in the strong feelings of family at the funeral, Amy asked Diddler Thorn, "What was my Granddaddy like?"

He got a very serious, respectful look on his face and said, "Bill Haines took care of his family. He was a saving man." That meant that he always had a little money laid away for his family.

Since my daddy died when I was eleven, my memories of

him are a mixture of what I know and what has been told to me. Over the years I have drawn a picture of him, added to it, erased parts of it, and still don't have it finished. The one important thing I know is that my mother loved him, and that tells me so much about what kind of man he was.

A few years ago my sister and I were sitting outside a store waiting for it to open and she said, "Naomi, do you know the most important thing that has ever happened to us?"

When I shook my head, she said, "The thing that has influenced our lives most is that our daddy loved our mother."

That simple truth explains so much of what I remember about my daddy, Bill Haines. When my mother got a job on Saturdays in Florence, thirty-five miles from Iuka, my daddy did not object. He was such an old-fashioned man, born in the eighteen hundreds, but with her, things were always different. I know that earlier she had sold mail-order dresses called the Hartford Frocks door-to-door, so this was not her first job. However, he seemed to be satisfied with her working, and for a traditional man, that seems unusual. It made her happy, and that was important to him. It is interesting to remember now that whenever I saw the softer, lighter side of my daddy, it was for my mother. He would laugh and tease her with little pet names like "Scootie Mae" for Eula Mae.

Several years ago, Mother gave me the bedroom furniture

that Daddy bought for them in the thirties. The set cost thirty-five dollars, but it carried with it the love and devotion he had for her. When I brought it to my home, I found where my daddy had written the date, place, and price of the set on the bottom of one drawer. The love he had for her became the soulplace of our home.

Since he worked long hours on construction and drove a long way to work, Saturday was the only day Daddy had to take care of his business. He paid all bills, bought groceries, and saved every penny of what was left. He was a tight man, whose financial goal was to provide for his family—no extras, but stable and steady.

We found out how true this was when Daddy was killed on the job in 1953, and Mother knew she would have to open his trunk and see where we stood financially. He had taken care of things, never burdening my mother with the details of our family finances. He was almost secretive regarding money, never spending foolishly, and seldom ever spending on himself. He soled his own shoes and pressed his own suit for church.

When Mother did open the trunk, she found a Rexall drugstore calendar for each of the last twenty-five years, individually rolled up with a rubber band. On the back of each month's sheet he had written every cent he had spent that month, down to the penny. Those calendars told a story themselves about a serious man whose first commitment was to family.

With the opening of the trunk, we all soon realized that out of meager wages he had saved enough to pay cash for our house the previous year. Even my mother did not know that until after he died.

Sometimes the only accurate way we know someone is through the eyes of others, especially when the person is quiet, or dies before we have time to really think about what we know about him.

When we moved to Iuka the second time, I learned something special about my daddy. I was in the fourth grade, and I had gotten my first bicycle at Christmas. I was suddenly free to roam, a freedom that has always been very important to me. I would often ride the six blocks from our house to downtown Iuka just to explore and look around. This freedom for a girl in the 1940s was truly unusual; of course it might be even more unusual today, when parents in some places are afraid to let their young children out of their sight even in their own front yards.

One day as I rode past my Aunt Dutch's house, I got a flat on my bike. I wheeled into the Standard Oil filling station and asked the man to fix it. He pulled the tube out of the tire, pumped it up it, and walked over to a tub of water. Turning the tube in the water, he watched for the bubbles to show the location of the puncture. When he had found it, he went in back of the filling station, put a hot patch on the hole, and returned to put the bicycle back together.

When he was finished, he looked at me and said, "That will be a nickel."

I said, "I don't have a nickel."

He asked, "Who's your daddy?"

With a sense of pride I told him, "My daddy's Bill Haines."

Without hesitation the man said, "I know Bill Haines. He'll pay me."

In some ways that says it all about Daddy.

~

Parents have an ongoing opportunity to teach and influence the next generation through their children. Sometimes parents claim they have lost their children to the streets, friends, TV, or other outside influences. I still believe that the single most influential person in a child's life is his parent, or parents. However, this is true only if parents choose to use this influence wisely, by *showing* a child how to live a healthy, productive life. Words alone just won't do it.

Not knowing my father well, I have depended on others to

help me complete a picture of him. The man they tell me about was a good man, and what I remember of him supports that image. His influence was still here after he was gone.

Moving Days

AFTER Daddy went to work for the Tennessee Valley Authority during the Great Depression, we moved around a lot, up and down the Tennessee River as he worked construction.

Until then, mostly in the twenties, he had farmed the land around the Haines place, and later he worked at the gravel pit over near the highway. But in the thirties the depression hit hard and ground the family down. There simply was no money. I know this was especially hard on my daddy, a proud and hardworking man who took care of his family. Mother told me that during this time Daddy would go down to the Whitehurst place after the cotton was picked and gather the stray bolls. He'd take that cotton to town and sell it to get a little money. Later on in Sunday School, I learned that what my daddy did was called gleaning in the Bible.

[handwritten margin notes: my Dad Had to quit school / In the 8th grade to Help support the family]

Thinking about that, I know that the depression must have been especially hurtful to Daddy. He had married Mother and taken her to live in a house on land he owned up above his homeplace. Mother reminds me that Daddy owned his own car when she married him in 1922. She would see him driving around Jaybird Park in Iuka in that car. She thought he was wonderful.

Before he went to work for the New Deal program called the Works Progress Administration—the WPA—and later TVA, things must have been hard. Mother said that after Daddy got the public works job, the first things they ordered from a catalog were a bedspread and a pair of khaki pants for him to wear. They had been using red clay to dye sheets for bedspreads.

When Daddy went to work for TVA, our lives must have really changed in some ways. Simply moving from the country to a series of houses in one small town or another was a big difference. In those years we did not have the word "migrant" or "migrant child" or I guess I would have been one.

Daddy was an oiler for the cranes and other heavy equipment. When he worked at Pickwick Dam in Tennessee or Kentucky Dam near Benton, Kentucky, he would pay attention to when the construction was nearing an end. Not wanting to be laid off, he would approach the foreman and ask for a transfer to the next job.

At least a half dozen times Daddy came home from work and announced, "I've been transferred." Then we all got busy getting ready to move. Daddy would borrow a truck to move our furniture and, in the early days, our cow. The only thing that was different about moving day was that we didn't cook and our bread came from the store. Mother always cooked biscuits for breakfast and cornbread for supper. But when we moved, Daddy would go to the store and buy a loaf of bread and a neck of bologna. That was all that was different.

Our house changed. Our neighborhood changed. I went to a new school. But nothing important really changed, because my daddy always worked hard, and he loved my mother. Though we moved a lot, our essential life stayed the same.

Shirley and I still listened to the mysteries on the radio on Sunday afternoons and ate crackers and drank water. We loved "The Shadow," "The Green Hornet," and "Intersanctum." I never really knew what that word meant, but when the Shadow laughed, I felt a tingle up my back and would look behind me.

During the week, at 6:30 each night, Daddy would turn on the radio to listen to Gabriel Heater's news commentary, the house would get still, and my sister Shirley and I would stand behind my daddy's chair and comb his hair with a fine-toothed comb while he listened.

Regardless of where we lived or how we got there, Mother

sat by me at night and listened to me read the Dick and Jane stories, watching me move the piece of paper under each line. Shirley and Lois taught me to add and subtract, and Mother got the woman up the street to give me my first permanent. Life was a continuous cycle of being cared for and cautioned.

No matter how many times we moved, home and my sense of my family and my place in it were always the same. Mother and Daddy saw to that.

∼

The ideal family or perfect family does not exist. It never did, except when we romanticize our pasts or believe in stories and books. The family, a microcosm of society, ebbs and flows with joy and pain, mistakes and successes. That flux is a given and is not why some families feel good while others don't.

Children think the world is like their own family. From infancy, each of us begins to chart our experience of the world, and this chart lives and breathes with family. If the family is a safe place, the world is a safe place. If the family is a violent, mean, unpredictable place, that is exactly what the child thinks the world must be.

Aunt Tennie's House

THERE was practically no such thing as rental property in 1945 when my Daddy was transferred to Pickwick Dam, but he wanted us to live in Iuka. Adding to our problem was the fact that many people did not want to rent to families with children. After failing to find a rental place, Daddy announced that we would just move into his Aunt Tennie's house.

My mother didn't seem too pleased with the idea, but there was no argument since there was no other way. We had to have a place to live. My folks always did what they had to do.

Aunt Tennie had died the year before, and her small, clapboard house stood empty out in the Snowdown community. To get there we went past the church to the next gravel road to the left. The little house had no electricity or running water. I don't think my children believe I really lived in that house because they think only Laura Ingalls Wilder did those things.

We owned a Warm Morning cast iron stove that burned coal. Daddy would buy coal by the ton and have it delivered, or, if he was short on money, he would buy it by the sack and bring it home himself. If he got a sack, it was a tow sack, a bag made of a loosely woven coarse fabric that others—depending on the part of the country where they lived—called a croaker sack or gunny sack.

He put the Warm Morning heater in Aunt Tennie's house to provide the only heat in the whole house except for the heat from the wood cook stove in the kitchen. Daddy would build a big fire in the mornings that would be tended all day, but allowed to burn down at night. We were used to sleeping in a cold house with lots of cover since it wasn't safe to have fire at night in those old, dry houses.

In the fall and spring the house would be warm all day from the heater and from the sunshine streaming through the windows. However, after bedtime the house would cool off and by the early morning hours, it would be really cold.

Sleeping in the front room, snuggled down into a feather bed, I would sometimes get restless in the night. Like all children, it was hard for me to get awake enough to really know what was the matter. Finally, after squirming around in the bed for a while, I would realize that I was cold.

I would cry out in the dark, "Mother, I'm cold!" My voice would echo through the quiet house and sound so loud in the cold stillness. Almost before I could get the word "cold" out of my mouth, I would hear feet hit the floor and footsteps come across the squeaky one-by-eight boards in that old house. Mother would stand a moment in the doorway of the room and then walk the two steps to the foot of my bed. I could not see her in the total darkness, but I could hear her breathe and feel her presence.

She would take the corners of an old patchwork quilt made from the dresses worn by my sisters and me and snap it out over the bed. I could feel the air swoosh in my face and smell our family as the old quilt settled over the bed and me.

Then in the darkness she would say, "Now you'll feel better." Of course I felt better because of the quilt, but I also felt better because she had brought it. She'd wrap her arms around me, and that scared, cold feeling would go away.

To cry in the night, to be afraid, to hear my own heart beat loudly, to be lonesome, and then to hear the footsteps of my mother was almost too much for words. I never look at that old quilt without remembering that feeling. Even now when life gets to be too much, I wrap myself in that old quilt with its cotton batting coming out at every seam and its every edge frayed.

Many years later as I slept on the floor beside my own sick child and leaned up to make sure he was breathing, I remembered Mother coming to me. I only wish that every child could cry out in the night and know that someone would come and wrap him up and say, "It's all right. I'm here."

~

Every child must believe that he or she is truly important to one person. Ideally this is a mother or father, but it has to be somebody. It never occurred to me that Mother would be too tired to come when I called in the night. I just knew she'd come because I knew I was that important to her.

Seeing her make sacrifices for me didn't register with me until I was an adult. It wasn't supposed to. Childhood is the only time in our lives that we should be able to take for granted such unconditional love and security. They should be taken for granted because childhood is a gift to be treasured that, in turn, can be given again to the next generation.

When MawMaw Haines Died

I guess the call came in the middle of the night. I really can't remember how we got word that MawMaw Haines was dying or even if we had a phone. (I do remember that at one time we had the number 39-J.)

We were living in Village Two, a company housing area for workers at the nearby Tennessee Valley Authority (TVA) plant and Wilson Dam. All the houses were alike except for size, and ours had two bedrooms. We lived on Dogwood Street, and the school bus driver teased me and called me Blondie every day when he picked me up. I was in junior high before I understood his joking reference to the comic strip.

I remember the hurrying around and getting ready to leave that night. Mother got me ready, pulling on dark corduroy pants under a gingham dress. She wrapped me in a quilt for the trip to Iuka since it was a cold, February night and she hoped I could sleep on the way. My sister Shirley gathered up some of her special things such as jacks, paper and pencil, and a book, perhaps thinking ahead to waiting and having to be quiet.

It was so dark, and the forty miles seemed like a long way. Mother and Daddy sat in the front of the '37 Chevrolet talking in quiet voices about what to expect. I really didn't understand anything about the situation because I hadn't seen death before. As I was "born late," both my grandfathers had died before I was born.

I realize now that in those days death was not really discussed. It was expected and endured. It was accepted. In those days there seemed to be a continuous mural of life and death instead of separate pictures that have to be explained and examined. Mother and Daddy understood why we were driving to Iuka that cold night.

Down Highway 72, over the Mississippi state line, there is a turnoff called Oldham. Sometimes I hear it pronounced "Old'am" now, but I know it is "Old Ham." I still don't understand why we cannot just accept the good of our past without trying to improve on it.

There was a store at Oldham where the local people bought kerosene, coffee, snuff, baking powder, sugar, and other things that they did not raise in their gardens. When we turned right at the store, we crossed a small creek which ran between the road and the railroad tracks. Later after my daddy died and I became the driver to Iuka, we would often stop and wade in that creek. Daddy, however, was a serious man, and I don't remember ever stopping with him.

The night MawMaw Haines died I don't remember Oldham or the creek. The darkness and the sadness pushed us along to the Snowdown turn. Turning right we moved slowly toward the Haines place. Daddy always drove slowly anyway, and I would sit with my chin resting on the top of the front seat between my parents' heads and watch the speedometer needle hover on thirty-five m.p.h. I don't think it ever occurred to me that a car could go any faster. That February night he seemed to drive even more slowly than usual. He wanted to get there to see her one more time, but he didn't want to get there to see her die.

As we neared the homeplace, some of the houses had lights in the windows. They had heard the news and were preparing food. Turning into the lane to the Haines place, I looked ahead and saw the windows of the house glowing with the softness of kerosene lamps. Several cars were pulled up in odd angles in the grove of oak trees around the place, but none were inside the small, dirt road that circled the house.

All was quiet and still. Daddy parked our car, and mother wrapped me up to carry me in the house. The quilt went with me. Shirley scrambled to get her things together, knowing that she would not be returning to the car for a long time.

We went in the back door which opened onto a screened back porch. Inside the kitchen, I was warmed with the familiar feel of the room where MawMaw had kept teacakes in a pie safe for the children and had poured buttermilk from a pitcher. People sat around the table in the kitchen, drinking coffee and talking quietly. Since we were close family, we all went directly to the front room to see MawMaw.

She lay in the big bed in the corner. She was a tiny woman who weighed around eighty pounds. She wore a size four shoe, the same size I wore at the time she died. Her good Sunday shoes, patent leather with a strap, became mine.

My Aunt Dutch and Uncle Jimmy were already there sitting around the bed. My daddy's other brother Whit and his son Benny lived on the homeplace with MawMaw and "took care of her," but I don't remember seeing them at all that night. They could have been outside with the men who were smoking on the front porch.

There was an "as usual" feeling in the room. The only thing different than any other time was that MawMaw was in the bed and not cooking and scurrying around. She lay quietly with her eyes closed. We walked over to look at her. She did not move. Mother and Daddy stayed there and waited.

Shirley had brought her jacks. We went out on the back

porch and played next to the high stacks of sugar which were ready to make wine. The small red rubber ball bounced on the wood floor and our hands gathered up the jacks and the continuous pictures of life and death came together in acceptance and comfort. That was my first time with death, and it seemed so much like life. MawMaw had gone, quietly, as she had lived. We saw death as but a single brushmark on a mural that intermingled with a game of jacks that two little girls played contentedly in the night.

∽

Looking back at my growing up years, I see always a pattern of predictability. MawMaw's death is an example of how life flowed evenly at our house. I just about always knew what to expect at home, and there weren't any big surprises. This feeling of predictability gives a strength and a security to our lives that makes it possible for us to deal with the upsets, uncertainties, and finally the undeserved pain that can destroy us.

Pal

WHEN we were living in what we called The Cracker Box, a shotgun-type house, my sister Shirley had a dog named Pal. He was part Chow and had a purple tongue. I hadn't started to school so I stayed home all day and played under the house. The little house was perched up on blocks with no underpinning. Shirley and Lois seemed to see more significance in that than I did.

One spring day while Shirley was at school, Pal and I played under the house most of the day. I had gathered bits of colored glass from the neighbors' trash pile, and I spent the day arranging them in the dirt like "playing house." Up in the morning when I went in the house, I took several bobby pins off Mother's dresser to play with outside. Sitting in the cool under the house it occurred to me that I could take those bobby pins and pin Pal's ears together. His ears were pointed and stood up straight, but I pulled them together and pinned them with about four pins, giving him a thoughtful and alert look.

We played the rest of the day together with his ears pinned. However, when Shirley came home from school and saw him, she was angry and upset. She reached out to take the pins off, but Pal growled and backed up. The ears were now sore and red around the pins, and he wouldn't let us touch him. While we waited on Daddy to return from work, Mother and Shirley just looked at me. Little was said.

When Daddy drove up in the yard late that afternoon and heard the news of Pal's situation, he stooped to see the chow crouched up under the house. Daddy walked up to the neighbor's house and asked him and his grown son to come down and help. Shirley, Mother, and I watched as the three grown men worked on Pal. Daddy pulled him from under the house. The two neighbors held him, one with his hand around his jaws, and my daddy pulled the bobby pins off. Everybody looked at me, but no one made a comment. There was nothing to say.

~

I didn't pin Pal's ears again, partly because I didn't want to hurt him, partly because I knew I had disappointed Mother, Daddy, and Shirley. There was no need for a switch, shouting, or other types of negative discipline. The greatest leverage on a child's behavior is the relationship the child has with the parents and other family members.

This relationship is forged from birth and fired with love. Some call it mutual respect. *However, I believe that children who are loved unselfishly and unconditionally really want to please their parents, more than anything else.*

We Called Her Miss Bama

NO one in Iuka, Mississippi, really knew Miss Florence Alabama Akers despite the fact they all thought they did. For sure, my daddy didn't know her that spring day in 1949 when he walked up on her porch and asked if we could rent an apartment in her house. He talked long and hard to her through the screen door, and she stepped outside and looked at me, shook her head, and stared again like I was a mad dog. Daddy continued to talk to her until she gave in, I guess, and agreed for us to move in.

She stood on the porch and watched his return to the car, never taking her eyes off me. She was dressed in a long, black skirt and a white blouse with a cameo pin at the throat. Her long, silver hair was plaited and laced tightly to the back of her head, and a row of short curls sat on her forehead. She was tall, bigger than my daddy, and in those days I thought my daddy was a giant.

When he got back to the car, he said to all of us, "She's never rented to children before." He didn't say it, but I knew what he meant, "Be good, be quiet, and stay out of trouble."

Called "Miss Bama" by everyone, Miss Akers had lived in and around Iuka all her life. She was both respected and feared by the people of the town. She was known for being tight with a dollar, driving a hard bargain, and holding her own with the men in town. She had never married, always supported herself, and stood as an object of mystery and curiosity. These feelings were mixed with a sense of awe because everyone thought she was rich. I guess each person had a different overall opinion, but one thing for sure, no one knew her, except maybe for us later on.

At eight years old I was a tomboy who could run faster, climb higher, and smoke more rabbit tobacco than anyone, especially my reserved, ladylike—Miss Bama's word—sister Shirley. We two were certainly thinking about different things that first day when we explored our part of her white, clapboard house, including a small central bathroom we shared with Miss Bama. There were no windows in the bathroom, and I know now that in the past it had been a big closet. It was lighted by a five-watt bulb hanging from the ceiling, and the light cast scary shadows over big stacks of the *Memphis Press-Scimitar* stored in two corners. I would learn quickly that turning off that light would be a very important part of my life. If I left it on, as I did many times, Miss Bama would knock on the door, frown down at me, and tell me I was wasting money.

Shirley and I nicknamed Miss Bama's black 1939 Chevrolet the "airplane." One Sunday afternoon a month Miss Bama would go out to the car, pull it up under the big water oak tree in the front yard, and "charge the battery." Partially deaf, she would crank the engine, rev it up, and sit there all afternoon. We would sit on the porch watching, knowing that if Miss Bama touched one more button in the car, it would lift off the ground and fly away.

Several weeks passed before Miss Bama warmed up to us and allowed us to come over on her side of the house. I think she was really interested in hearing about Shirley's activities at Iuka High School, especially news about boyfriends and dates. She asked me, too, but only out of manners. Later on she really got involved in Shirley's teenage dating life, pushing some beaus and sulking about others.

I loved to go on her side because the sights and smells were like no other I'd known. Miss Bama had five rooms of heavy, mahogany antique furniture. I knew that because Mother and Daddy discussed it. Dozens of pictures of people in beards and plaits hung in gold frames on the walls, and under a piece of glass on the coffeetable were more Kodak pictures. There were thick black velvet rolls with flowers and birds sewed on them in front of all the doors. The house smelled like turpentine and furniture oil, yet old and dusty.

After she got used to us, she told us of her days as the postmistress of Allsboro, Alabama, a small rural community just over the state line where her family owned farmland. She took us with her to visit the tenants and sharecroppers on her land, packing us in the "airplane." While Miss Bama and Shirley talked about boys, I sat in the back seat, stared out the rear window, and watched the endless tracks of Miss Bama's tires on the wet pavement. Unlike the tracks my daddy's car left, the center line ran exactly in the middle between Miss Bama's tracks; this was an impressive sight to an eight-year-old.

When we arrived in Allsboro to visit the small, unpainted tenant houses, Miss Bama would always ask to see any new baby. She would draw the mosquito netting aside and place a shiny, new quarter in the tiny, wrinkled hand. I had never seen a black baby, mosquito netting, or that many shiny quarters before.

My visits to "the other side" became regular as Miss Bama became used to having us around, and we weren't so scared of her. She would let me help make jam, can beans, and even make applesauce. My job was to place the cooked apples in a cone-like strainer and push the sauce through the holes with a fat stick.

One day when we were working, a knock came at the kitchen door. Miss Bama opened the door and let in the delivery man from the grocery store with a metal box filled with pickling salt, canning jars, and dill weed. In those days you could order your groceries from the home-owned store, and a delivery man would bring them out in an open green metal box. When Miss Bama looked at the man, he seemed uncomfortable as he stood waiting for her to pull out two one-dollar bills and a quarter from her purse. He glanced around the room and spotted a brown whiskey bottle on a high shelf. I knew it was a whiskey bottle because my mother had seen it and told me.

Since all of Mississippi in 1949 was "dry" (no liquor sales allowed), the man looked at the bottle a long time. Miss Bama baited him and said, "Would you like a little sip, Bud?" Without a word, the man reached up, grabbed the bottle, uncorked it and took a long swallow. He gasped, coughed, and sputtered, realizing too late it was apple cider vinegar. He rushed out the door, cursing under his breath. Miss Bama's only comment was, "Men never learn better." I think Miss Bama was an early women's libber.

In the fall of 1950 my daddy had to have kidney stones removed and the nearest big hospital was in Memphis, Tennessee. Mother arranged for Shirley and me to stay with Miss Bama since school was still going on. I am sure that we were the only children to ever stay in her part of the house.

She cooked for us, making her special treats. The first day it was a white layer cake with sweetened tomatoes for icing. I ate the cake part and stuffed the icing in the pockets of my school dress to be hidden outside later. She also cooked spinach and cracked raw eggs over the top for what she called "garnish". The yolks slid to the edge of the bowl and pooled up where I could eat around them, which was good because they would have leaked in my pocket. The usual nightly meal was something she called "mush," made by slowly dusting corn meal into boiling water and thickening it. Many evenings she would eat mush for supper, pulling her chair up to the stove and using the oven door as a table. I would sit and stare in fascination as she removed her teeth after the meal, licked them off, and put them back in place. I had never seen teeth come out before.

Many days passed with my parents away, and Miss Bama was always in charge. She had me sleeping on a day bed in the front room which she had piled high with twelve (I counted them) old musty patchwork quilts. When they were all in place, their weight kept me from turning over. One night I made a serious mistake. I coughed. Miss Bama heard me, and rumbled into the room with a long, wool scarf and a jar of Penetro Rub. She unrolled the scarf and carefully spread the salve over its entire length. She pulled me from the covers, wound the scarf round and round my neck, and returned me to the gingham, calico and unbleached domestic. With a look of satisfaction, she said, "That will take care of a cough." It did. No sound could have gotten out of my throat, and I was afraid to cough anyhow.

It snowed on Thanksgiving weekend in Iuka the year we stayed with Miss Bama. On Monday, with snow on the ground, she searched through her closet to find a pair of gray galoshes that I would use to cover my shoes for the walk to school. They were made for old lady shoes with block heels, and Miss Bama had torn one of them up the back seam on some snowy day in the past. She pulled them from the closet, took purple thread, sewed up the rip, and stood watching while I put them over my brown Girl Scout school shoes. One block down the street, I took the galoshes off and hid them under a bush. In Miss Bama's care, I found that silence and secret solutions were always the best.

One cold night I was sleeping in that front room, which was actually a front hall. That put me right by the front door. Shirley had gone on a date with a boy named Bill. Miss Bama did not favor this beau, and was sulled up at Shirley for going. They left at 6:00 in the evening, and she had told Shirley to be home no later than 8:30. Beginning around 8:00, Miss Bama was pacing through the house muttering, "Where in the world is she?"

By 8:25 she had worked herself up into a frenzy, going out on the front porch and letting the freezing wind blow through that hall. At about 8:30 she walked out on the porch and said, "I'm going to call Chunky Chambers." I knew that was the sheriff, and I was really scared. As she stormed through the house, I heard the car drive up and shouted, "They're home!" I think Miss Bama was disappointed that she didn't get to sic the sheriff on Bill.

The day before my parents returned from Memphis, my good friend Judy and I walked home from school to find the "airplane" missing from the driveway. When we reached the porch, we could hear the telephone ringing in Miss Bama's side. Our family didn't have a phone, and I just knew it was my mother, but stood helplessly on the long porch, unable to get inside Miss Bama's locked part of the house. Judy ran to the garage and returned with a key from a vienna sausage can. We tried it on the door lock, but it would not budge. Finally, we decided to remove the screen from the big window of Miss Bama's living room and raise the window sash. Just as Judy was stepping inside, I heard the roar of Miss Bama's car as she turned up the driveway. We both froze in fear as the phone stopped ringing. Miss Bama covered the big yard in a half-dozen strides, grabbed Judy by the leg, and pulled her from the window. She told Judy to leave and never come back, herded me into the house, and told me, "That girl is trouble." When I've seen Judy since at Showdown, we've laughed and agreed that Miss Bama acted like a true mother that day, never seeing my part in the incident.

I see now that the year we lived at Miss Bama's not only gave me a unique look at the life of one of Iuka's legendary characters, but it gave Miss Bama an opportunity, probably her only opportunity, to invest herself in the life of a child. Our lives touched briefly, but I gathered a tow sack full of memories, many exciting and dramatic, but all a testimony to how a crusty recluse showed her love to a child.

∼

Much to my surprise, people who know me well say that I'm getting more like Miss Bama every day. I think that means that I enjoy my own company, feel free to be myself, relish a challenge, and can be pretty hardheaded. If that's true, that statement translates into (1) love for solitude, (2) self-confidence, (3) assertiveness, and (4) tenacity. These contemporary characteristics that we desire in children are the very ones that I associate with being a "menopause baby." My parents did a good job in letting Naomi be Naomi.

The Memphis Haineses

WHETHER we recognize it or not, grown-ups have a powerful influence on children. We as adults sometimes forget that a word, a sentence, a smile, a conversation, an action, something so simple in passing that we don't even think about its significance, can be special in the life of a child.

On the days that we would go to Snowdown Methodist Church for Homecoming, there would be a real coming to-gether of kinfolks who had not seen each other for a long time. There would be a lot of people from all over north Mississippi, Alabama, and Tennessee, and a few that would come from many miles away. Just seeing each other and renewing those ties were a very special part of Snowdown.

When I was a child, an incident that happened each year at Snowdown made a tremendous impact on my life. Like so many things that happen to a child, I didn't realize the significance of it at the time, but over the years I came to see what an influence there was in a short conversation with someone I hardly knew.

We would serve our plates at the long tables under the trees. Most everybody stood up to eat except for the very old people, and straightbacked chairs would be brought out from the church for them to sit on. I would go down the wooden table and fill up my plate, and each year about the time I'd get to the end of that table, something very special would happen. There would be a little sense of expectancy or electricity in the crowd—everybody twittering and talking to each other—and out of that, I would hear folks say, "Look, look, it's the Memphis Haineses."

With a sense of awe, the crowd would stop and look as this big fine car, Cadillac Sedan De Ville, would pull up in the yard of the church and down to the end of the table. The Memphis Haineses were the part of my family that went off and made some money. Daddy said they made a tow sack full of money. They got into business in Memphis during a boom time and became wealthy, by Snowdown's standards, for sure. The car would pull up to the end of that table and I would be standing there, six years old, in the dress Mother had made me, my Sunday dress, holding my plate. Out of that car would step my daddy's cousin, Armistead Haines, from Memphis, Tennessee.

I was struck dumb. He was the first man I ever saw whose pants would stay up on their own. My daddy had always worn pants with a belt and suspenders or galluses, all trussed up, but this man wore magic pants that stayed up on their own. I would be standing there as a little girl looking right at his waist, thinking that any second they were going to come down. I was absolutely amazed by his pants.

He would get out of that car and go around to its trunk and open it up, and every year he would have in that trunk a wooden case of Coca-Colas. They were those little six-and-a-half-ounce Coca-Colas, you know, and there were twenty-four of them. The only time I would see twenty-four Cokes was at Snowdown when Armistead Haines would pull them out of the trunk and set them on the end of the table.

He would turn around and see me standing there, and would walk those two steps toward me and look down and ask me two questions. He asked me the same two questions every year. He'd look down and say, "Whose girl are you?"

I'd look up and say, "I'm Eula's girl."

He would smile and say, "Oh, you're Eula's girl."

I would stand up a little taller. "Yes, I'm Eula's girl."

Then this man whom everybody respected would smile, a look of approval on his face. I had a feeling inside me of being connected with somebody this man approved of, and it didn't have anything to do with the years she had gone to school or the money she had made. The respect in his voice was because he knew she was a *good woman*.

I could change the world if every child could feel what I felt standing there those hot July days. I could stand up in front of a man people respected and I could tell him I was Eula's girl, and he would have that smile on his face. If every child could have that sense of being connected to a person like that, to be able to say "I'm Eula's girl," with that response, we would change the lives of children in every way.

The second question he asked me was the one that we ask children when we really don't know what else to say. It's a filler. It's one we ask children in doctor's offices when we're sitting there by them and feel like we have to say something.

Armistead Haines would look down at me and say, "Well, what are you going to be when you grow up?"

The first year I told him I was going to be a missionary. I could just see myself over in Africa, floating down the Congo River in a big dugout canoe with natives sitting up front with big branches. They would be fanning me, and the drums would be beating. I'd have the Bible under my arm, going out into the wilderness to save the heathens I'd heard about in Sunday School. I was just so full of myself I could hardly stand it. I was going to be a missionary.

This man I hardly knew looked at me and said, "You can do it. You can do it."

I think the next year I told him I wanted to be an archeologist. I didn't know what it was, but he didn't, either, so it didn't matter.

When I told him I wanted to be an archeologist, he said, "You can do it."

The year I remember most was the year that he asked me and I told him I wanted to be a teacher. Teachers are the most respected people in my family. My mother has always said that they have a calling next to a preacher. Since I gave up teaching, my mother has never understood what I have been doing. Whatever she thinks of my work, she certainly does not hold it in as high esteem as teaching.

There were many teachers in my family. My aunts went to school in the summers to get their teaching certificates at Mississippi State College, Ole Miss, and Mississippi State College for Women. My sister Shirley had a career teaching Latin and Spanish. I always knew that teachers were important in my family.

But when I revealed my ambition that year to Armistead Haines, he didn't know I had a secret reason for wanting to be a teacher. I thought that if you were a teacher you got *unlimited* school supplies. I thought there was a great cabinet somewhere that teachers could go to, and they could open it anytime, and it would be filled with Blue Horse paper, tablets, lots of pencils that still had erasers, those big pink erasers that were pink on one end and gray on the other, and those big block erasers that left hunks on the page.

But most important of all, in that cabinet there would be a box of thirty-six crayons. I always wanted thirty-six crayons so much. That was the kind of box where you pulled back the lid and the crayons were arranged in stair-stepped rows, and there was a sharpener on the back. In that special box the crayons had their colors written on the side, and I wanted azure so much, along with indigo, flesh, and lime. But all I ever got was a box of flat eight.

Something about school supplies is very special to children. The smell of them and the feel of them go along with the feeling of starting over every year, of having a clean slate on which to begin. I love school supplies even now, and I think most of us do. The feel and smell of crayons is particularly special.

When I told Armistead Haines that I wanted to be a teacher, he looked right at me and said, "You can do it."

Over those years, each incident with Armistead Haines lasted about two or three minutes, but they made a real difference in my life because, see, I believed him. Now my mother gave me that feeling, my sisters gave me that feeling, and then added in was the confidence I got from Armistead Haines. When this man who was held up high by the Snowdown community said to me as a young girl, "You can do it," I believed him. That little time and effort makes a big difference in the life of a child. If he's still alive, he probably doesn't even remember.

～

No contact with a child is insignificant. It either has a positive outcome or a negative outcome. Not much is neutral with children. As adults and parents and extended family, especially, we should never forget that those little five-minute and ten-minute periods we have with children can be a real boost to their sense of themselves, their feelings of worth and value. The encouragement, the possibilities they feel, the confirmation of that interaction all go together to push a child forward and to give him or her a sense of direction, but, more importantly, a sense of hope.

One Christmas in the Village

BEING tight with money was a way of life in my family. Mother said Daddy never wanted to be like the man who lived out from Iuka who needed a new hoe handle, but didn't even have the dime to buy it. Money was always used either for things we had to have, or saved for the future. There was no other category for my Daddy.

When we lived in Village Two in Sheffield, Alabama, Daddy was working at Wilson Dam, and Mother worked on Saturdays as an extra in Barham's Dry Goods Store. I went to the first, second, and part of the third grades at Annapolis Avenue School.

The Christmas I was in first grade I had seen a Mickey Mouse ring in the Sears catalog and told Mother I wanted it for Christmas. It cost about five dollars. At that time I didn't realize that for both my parents, their childhood Christmases were celebrated with an orange in their stocking. That had been Santa to them.

On Christmas Eve that year, Mother worked late at Barham's, and Daddy picked her up and brought her home. I was really excited about Christmas and went to bed early. Later on I heard Mother and Daddy talking in the kitchen.

She said, "You mean you didn't get what I told you to get for Naomi?"

I couldn't hear his exact words, but I knew it meant he hadn't. They talked a long time, and she was upset. Finally, I heard her get up and get her purse. She rustled in the purse and walked over and took the stocking down. I could barely see her through the tiny slit in the door.

I lay awake a long time thinking about it. I was hurt, confused, and disappointed.

The next morning the five dollars she had earned at Barham's on Christmas Eve was in my stocking. Mother never even commented on it. Both Mother and Daddy did what they thought should be done.

That Christmas I first felt disappointed and then unexpectedly rich. Later, I felt guilty for taking her Christmas Eve pay and angry at him for not wanting to spend the money. Now, I understand how members of a family work together, sometimes wrong, sometimes right, but generally taking up slack for each other.

~

I have seen some of the most hurtful events at Christmas. At a time when Southerners, especially, treasure the nostalgia of this season, we are so vulnerable to loss, aloneness, and change. We are acutely aware of our need, our limitations, our pain. For this reason, children must have access to open discussions with the adults in their lives, attention and affection, involvement in family rituals, and *not* just gifts and material things. Christmas, like any other part of the year, should be a renewal of our love for each other.

Country Funerals

IT seems like I always went to funerals. Beginning with my grandmother's, I was carried to the funerals of many relatives, almost always at Snowdown in the cemetery behind the little church and enclosed by a fence and gate.

The ritual would have actually started two days earlier when the body was taken back home after preparation by the funeral home. Taking the body home was a part of how we did things back then. I suppose now it seems strange, almost morbid, but then it was the natural, respectful thing to do. The casket would be set in a place of honor in the living room or front room. The casket was open, and we all walked around it, stood by it, and visited with each other as if the person in the casket was a part of the gathering. It felt right and comfortable.

All of the friends and neighbors would bring food for the family. The kitchen table would be covered with fried chicken, egg custard pie, and butter beans. It would all be laid out to eat whenever the family felt like it. Quiet, reserved friends set out plates, cleared away used dishes, and poured coffee. After a while a cloth was spread over the food, signaling that dinner was over. However, if a new person came in, he was always welcome to pull back the tablecloth and eat.

While the body was at home, there was always someone awake to attend it, hence, the term "wake." The men took the late hours, talking quietly, smoking, and telling stories, often about their times with the person who had died. Late at night, the people sitting up would return to the kitchen to eat again. The cloth would be removed, and clean plates set out. I'm sure the mourners were hungry, but it also passed the time in the early morning hours.

This was a familiar process, a ritual that drew loose ends together. The relative who had died was a part of it. I remember seeing my mother bend down over the casket in our living room and give my father a kiss on his forehead. It felt right then, and it still does. I know some people would say that it taints their feeling about the house, the room, the place, but the way it was done back then, I just don't remember it that way.

At tiny Snowdown Methodist Church the funeral music was usually provided by the church choir. The sharp notes of the old upright piano played, "When the Roll Is Called Up Yonder," and the choir added their feelings to the moment. The tinny sound of the old piano blended in with the "country alto" so common to small church choirs. It was slow and mournful, but right.

At my daddy's funeral, a Mrs. Woodley from the Iuka church sang "When They Ring Those Golden Bells." I think Aunt Dutch arranged that, perhaps thinking it would be more sophisticated for her brother's funeral. Dutch lived in town, and I suppose she thought Snowdown needed to be more like town. I've always wondered if my mother would have been happier with the choir.

After the funeral, we would move out into the cemetery, pallbearers carrying the casket. As a child I remember the small graves of children covered with mussel shells, the graves with rocks for markers, the grave with a picture of a soldier caught in time and frozen forever, and the fence around the graves of my great-grandparents. I always wondered what the fence was for or who it was to keep out.

In those years it was customary to scrape off the graves and keep the red clay bare like the yards of my relatives, swept clean with a broom, showing care and attention. Grass was not welcome and not tolerated.

As we walked through the cemetery, Mother would say, "Watch out, Naomi, don't step on that grave. We don't step on graves." I would always jump when she would say that. I felt that respect, yes, but I also felt a fear that the person would know. It was hard to know when I was walking on a grave since they were in no particular lines, and some had stones at the head and some at the feet. It is still hard for me to tell.

After the service in the church, or the "house" as it was called, we would gather around the new grave. In later years, the funeral home would put up a tent over the grave, but mostly I remember just being out there in the open. The immediate family would stand close to the casket, and the extended family behind them. Friends circled the outside. There was an unspoken but understood order to the ritual. Closest people to the immediate family stood nearer to the grave. If it was a Masonic funeral, the Masons would stand in their white leather aprons and chant strange words that sounded like, "So modid be." Then the preacher would read the Bible and pray. Afterwards he would go down the line, shake the hands of the family, and step away.

The family would slowly rise and move away from the grave. They would huddle a few feet away while the grave was being filled, pretending not to hear the dirt hit the coffin. When the dirt was in place and the flowers were placed on the grave, the family would return to look and talk about their grief and their memories.

Maybe the treatment of death says the most about my people. It was respectful, loving, and comfortable. The cemetery was a good place, a place that was familiar because my people were there.

Now we have placed death in a faraway place where our children cannot see it. It is something to fear, to deny. Somehow my people were able to see it for what it is, a part of life. They had learned that lesson well, through diphtheria, smallpox, and pneumonia. Every family plot had at least one child's tiny grave, a child that will forever be small and innocent. One cousin's family plot has the graves of four tiny infants lined up with tiny white crosses.

One day my children will take me back to Snowdown for the last time. They will feel at home that day, and I will too.

~

Watching my mother take care of her aging mother taught me how to take care of her. It's just that simple. I know what to do because she showed me. Also, watching my mother grieve with others, take food, send cards, and sit quietly at the side of the family have all taught me how to deal with death and responsibility. One thing I admire about African-American families is how they take care of their old people. So many times I've heard them say, "All of the grandchildren take nights about taking care of their Grandma." Nursing homes, memorial services, the fragmented extended family, and modern ideas about "sparing" children all seem to have changed the routine of death. This change is not an improvement to me.

English Peas

BEING "born late" I pretty much got things my way. Mother overlooked a lot, was very accepting of me, let me get dirty playing, and didn't nag me about grades or homework. She just let me be Naomi.

The only vegetable I really liked growing up was spinach. Now that was unusual because we did not grow it in the garden. However, since she really believed that I had to have a least one green vegetable each day, she cooked spinach every night. We just didn't have a hassle about it. Once a week she'd buy a can of Del Monte spinach and give me a big spoonful every night. I would feel so special when she gave me that spinach just because she knew I liked it.

In those days, Mother would make all of my clothes the week before school started. She would get out the old treadle machine, basically use one pattern (probably Simplicity 1216), and make me several dresses out of various ginghams and prints. Each had a round collar that she called a Peter Pan collar made of white pique, two pockets in front, and a sash that tied in the back. Mother absolutely hated to sew, and those days were pretty miserable as she fought that old machine, and it usually won. In the meantime I just stayed outside and out of her way.

Later she would take me to the Florence shoe store and buy me a pair of Girl Scout shoes—brown lace-up oxfords that were made of iron so the only way to get rid of them was to grow out of them or die.

That first year, Mother plaited my hair into two pigtails, one standing out on each side of my head. With my new dress and shoes, she had me ready for first grade, and I believed, as she did, that I was the only first grader in town.

When I got to school, my teacher was Mrs. Hovater from Barton, and she told us all about the rules. She said that ol' Miss Solomon (I thought that was all one word) was in charge of the lunch room and wouldn't let us out until we had eaten all of our food.

That first day of school, when I got to the lunchroom, there on my plate was a whole wad of big, tough English peas. To make things worse their juice was running into the mashed potatoes. They weren't the young, tender LeSeur kind of peas. These were so big that one side caved in, and when you bit into one, it exploded in your mouth. I sat there the entire lunch period trying to decide what to do because ol' Miss Solomon was checking plates. I finally picked up the whole pile of peas and put them in my pocket, slipped out of my seat and marched past Miss Solomon with my clean plate.

I went out to the playground. By then the juice from the peas had run down my dress, leaving a slick green stream all the way to the hem. I could mash the hem between my fingers and it would squoosh. I found a rock and hid the peas under it.

By the time I got home, the pea juice had dried out and my dress stuck out with a green smear down the front. Mother took one look at me and said, "What happened to you?"

I said, "We had peas."

That was all that needed to be said. After that, every time I went home in that shape, Mother would look at me and say, "Well, I see you had peas today."

~

When I visited my mother last year, she was taking a nap. I crawled up on the bed beside her and I put my head on the pillow next to my ninety-six year-old mother. I love to feel the warmth of her even now, and I still put my head in her lap if I can.

That day we lay there for a while and then I asked, just like it hadn't been fifty years, "Mother, why did you cook that spinach for me every night growing up?"

She waited a while, and then said, "Baby, I just didn't see any sense in making you miserable over that."

Rolling Cigarettes

DADDY rolled his own cigarettes. This was long before the Tobacco Enlightenment Period when we found out smoking would kill us. It was just a part of our lives like any other. My children question me now about this tobacco story, but they can never understand how much it was an accepted part of my life.

On Sunday afternoons in the summer, Daddy would get a brown paper sack and tear it open to make a big sheet. He and I would sit on the front porch and mix his tobacco. In town the day before he would have purchased a sack of Country Gentleman and a can of Prince Albert. He liked to mix these two together to make his own blend.

I was honored to have the job of running my fingers through the tobacco to make sure it was thoroughly mixed. Then he would pack it in the Prince Albert can to carry to work that next week. It was really a special and important time for me to work with him on the tobacco even though we didn't talk much. It's a reminder to me now that even the most insignificant event with a child, even one that would now be considered mundane, can be the tenderest.

I would watch closely as Daddy rolled a cigarette. He would take the thin cigarette paper and place the index finger of his left hand in the middle, making a half cylinder. Then he would carefully tap the sack of tobacco, allowing a few leaves at a time to fall on the paper, back and forth until there was an even row of tobacco. Then he would take one string of the sack of Country Gentleman in his teeth and one in his right hand and draw the sack opening together. Placing the sack beside him, he was now free to adjust the tobacco in the paper, roll it from both ends, hold it firmly, and lick the exposed edge. Then he would press down the wet edge to make it stick, the wetness of his saliva coming through. With a flourish, he would take one end and pinch it together. The cigarette was ready to smoke.

It was a process that fascinated me. Soon I could roll a cigarette, too, although I was not allowed to strike a match, much less smoke a cigarette.

Mother didn't smoke except once in a while. If we were going to Iuka for a singing at Spring Park, for example, or anywhere special, Daddy would buy a pack of "ready rolls," usually Camels. Then on the way to Iuka, when he would light his, he would give Mother one, and she would smoke it. It was just something else they did together that was special. We loved to see her smoke that one cigarette.

Being "born late," I had a sense of freedom, daring, and general adventure in my nature. Mother would often smile, as others would, and say "Well, you know Naomi. She was born late." For years, I had no idea what that meant, but I did know that I was free in the world and everyone cut me a lot of slack.

With that sense of freedom, I would routinely gather up the butts that had been thrown away around the yard and hoard them until I had enough to roll my own cigarette. For two or three years I just rolled them to see if I could, never smoking them. Striking a match was forbidden.

However, when I was about eight years old, I was sweeping the floor and accidentally swept a match and it struck. With the striking rule made moot, I was free to roll and smoke, an activity that I absolutely loved.

When we lived at Miss Bama's house, Mother was working in Florence at Barham's Dry Goods Store. She would ride the bus from Iuka to Florence early Saturday morning, and then Daddy would go up later in the day to get groceries and pick her up after work.

When he went up to Florence on Saturday to pick her up, he would leave Shirley and me at home to clean the house. We would usually have about fifty cents to go to town and spend for lunch. I remember the first hamburger I ever saw at Jim Timbs's hamburger stand in Iuka. They were a nickel each, and we would buy six and two R.C. colas. Life was good.

One Saturday morning we had been working on the house and I finally had my part done. I had waited all week for this time. I had been saving up cigarette butts to be ready for Saturday. I slipped outside behind the old tin garage, sat down on the ground, leaned up against the back of the garage, and proceeded to roll the best cigarette ever.

For my special project, I had saved a large brown grocery bag which I opened up to its full size. I emptied the tobacco from many cigarette butts onto the open sack and began to roll a cigarette at least twelve or fourteen inches long. When I got it rolled, I bit the edge of the paper, a special technique I had learned to make the brown paper stick better, and stuck it down. Then I pinched the wad of brown paper at one end, to hold the tobacco in. I was ready.

I slowly leaned back, took a big kitchen match, reached back over my shoulder, and drew it down the rough tin of the garage wall. The match flared, and I touched it to the end of the long cigarette. My short eight-year-old arms barely reached the end of the long cigarette. All the brown paper pinched at the end flamed up brightly and then settled to a glow. I took my first puff.

A voice over my left shoulder was like a bolt of thunder. Shirley said smugly, "I've got you this time. I'm telling Mother as soon as she gets home."

"Please don't tell Mother," I begged. "I'll do anything you say if you just won't tell Mother."

Shirley's eyes narrowed and she said, "All right, from now on you must do everything I say or I'm telling. We'll have a secret password, and when I say that word, you better do what I say or I'm telling. The word will be DOG. When I say DOG, you better jump." She said "daawgh" and made the word last forever.

For the next several months my life was miserable. Shirley would say, "Get me a drink of water."

I'd say, "Get it yourself."

She'd whisper in such a threatening voice, "DOG, Naomi." Shirley could make the one syllable of the word sound like a sentence. I would scramble to please and make her happy. It was a nightmare.

As with all blackmail, the day came when the telling was

worse than the threat of punishment. We were sitting in the kitchen, and Mother was at the stove frying corn in a black iron skillet. Shirley said, "Bring me some milk."

I said, "Get it yourself."

She mouthed, "DOG", her eyes adding a lot more.

I just couldn't stand it anymore, and I yelled, "Just tell her and get it over with."

My heart was beating fast when Shirley turned to Mother and said, that voice reserved for tattling on your sister, "Mother, Naomi has been smoking."

Mother laid down the spoon, turned around to me, looked straight into my eyes and said in a quiet voice, "Naomi, have you been smoking?" Her eyes were disappointed and hurt.

I lowered my head and twisted in the chair as I did many times, and said, "Yes, I have." Her look hurt me so much.

"Naomi, I wish you wouldn't do that anymore," she said, looking into my soul, and then she turned back to the stove. She said nothing else. She didn't have to. She loved me, and I couldn't stand to hurt her. I don't smoke today.

∼

It took me years to realize the most significant characteristic about my mother as a parent. She was able to see each of her children as an individual with different personalities and needs, and then build a unique relationship with each one. I realize even now that my conversations with her are different from those she has with my sisters, and her expectations of me are also different from what she expects of them. She knows what I can and cannot do.

Learning What Smart Really Is

LOOKING back over my childhood, I see a series of events that shaped my understanding about what it means to be smart or not so smart. None alone means very much, but collectively, they say so much about the impact that adults have on how we feel about ourselves.

When I went to first grade, I could already read, write, add, and subtract. It was not a miracle, just the result of my sisters' instruction. Shirley, five and a half years older, and Lois, eighteen years older, worked with me, teaching me what I should learn at school. As a result of this attention, I was in trouble at school from the first day—Mrs. Hovater just didn't know what to do with me.

We sat in double desks and my partner was Mary Ginny Curry. I was always squirming and talking since I had already learned the alphabet and numbers. I tormented everyone around me, especially Mary Ginny and Edward, a redheaded boy who sat in front. The early part of the year I was satisfied looking at the back of Edward's head because with his hair slicked down, I could see a wide, flat place unlike anything I had ever seen. It was a little like he had been hit with the iron Mother heated to press clothes.

However, as the days passed, I talked, got out of my seat, and looked out the window. Finally, not knowing what else to do, Mrs. Hovater kissed me, hugged me, told me she loved me, and put me in the cloakroom. The cloakroom ran across the length of the front of the classroom with a door on each side. In the cloakroom were hooks for coats and a place to put lunches. My hook would contain my coat and a pair of green corduroy pants that Mother insisted I wear under my dress to keep my legs warm on the way to school.

I amused myself in the cloakroom by singing to myself and looking in lunch sacks, sampling the peanut butter and banana sandwiches wrapped in waxed paper. I never felt rejected or scorned by anyone, certainly not Mrs. Hovater. She just accepted me the way I was. She understood why I got in trouble, and she handled it the only way she knew. I saw Mrs. Hovater in later years when I was in college and she was back working on her graduate degree. I still loved her, and she remembered me, and loved me.

My fourth grade teacher at Annapolis Avenue School gave me a different feeling about smart. On the last day of school my teacher said to the class, "I'm going to call out each of your names. I want you to line up around the wall in the order I call your name."

We followed her instructions, and soon the entire class was standing around three of the walls. I silently stood there and looked down the line at the faces I had come to know.

Then she said, "I have lined you up from the smartest to the dumbest."

I looked at that line slowly all the way to the end. My eyes met the girl who was last. I looked away. Even at nine, I knew something terrible had happened, and I was embarrassed.

Later, that same teacher took several of us to a Sheffield High School track meet where her son was a member of the team. He didn't really do anything special but run a few laps. Afterwards, the teacher said, "He'll get a nice gift for that good performance." I wondered why she didn't feel the same kindness toward that last girl in the line who was also trying.

The threat of polio reached an all-time high in 1952. During the summers of the polio scare, the swimming pool at Spring Park in Tuscumbia was closed. Everyone was afraid of getting polio but didn't know what to do to stop it. I had joined Girl Scouts by then, and we all went to the day camp in the park.

We had nature studies each day where we talked about animals and plants of Alabama. I really didn't know a lot about Alabama since I had lived mostly in Mississippi, Tennessee, and Kentucky. However, each day we had a contest where there would be a question and the first five people to answer the nature question correctly got a prize.

The last day the question was, "What is the state flower of Alabama?" I had no idea, but I hung around and watched people come up and whisper their answers in the leader's ear. Three people got it right, and when a fourth whispered in the lady's ear, I heard the answer, *goldenrod.*

The leader said, "That's four."

Not hesitating, I walked up and whispered, "goldenrod."

She said, "Right, Naomi."

I got the last prize, a yo-yo, and I never forgot the Alabama state flower.

Another prize I got for getting the right answer, this one a bit more deserved, came from my Uncle Howard, who was a traveling salesman. He drifted in and out of our lives as he lived in many places across the country. He was a handsome man with black hair and dark eyes, and he dressed up a lot and drove a big car. Despite being born in Iuka like everyone else, he didn't talk like we did. He had what we called a "northern brogue," and it made him sound sharp and unfriendly.

One summer when Howard visited us on his way some-where, we all were sitting in the living room while the adults talked. Mostly Howard talked and bragged about how much money he made.

Out of nowhere, he looked at me smugly and said, "I've been in almost all the states. Naomi. If you can name all the states in twenty minutes, I will give you twenty dollars."

This was about 1951, and twenty dollars was a fortune. I jumped up and got a piece of paper. He looked at his watch, but he never thought for one minute that I could do it. He was just showing off for the family, being a big man.

I sat down and began to write. I got ten, then twenty, then thirty, and forty. Finally, I had forty-seven, and time was running out. At last I thought of the last one, Wyoming. I had it *and* him.

Howard looked upset, then almost angry, but he was caught. All of the adults were looking at him. He begrudgingly took out his billfold and handed me the twenty-dollar bill. We were always uncomfortable with each other after that. I didn't like him much, and he didn't like me.

I used that twenty dollars to buy a record player to play the Hit Parade songs such as "You Belong to Me" and "Rags to Riches." I borrowed the records from Brenda Geise who lived up the street. Later, after several years I sold the record player to a neighbor for fifteen dollars. Howard's money, promised for knowledge, was well spent.

When I went to Wyoming, fly-fishing and camping, I remembered the challenge that Howard had made to a fifth grader. He probably didn't think I was very smart, and he certainly didn't mean to help me be smarter.

Experts tell us that we are born with a certain I.Q., and that it doesn't change much over our lives. I was given an I.Q. test in first grade, and another in the eighth. When my I.Q. jumped fifteen points, the teacher was amazed. However, our experiences allow us to take our basic abilities and use them better.

~

As a child I couldn't play the piano or sing, do gymnastics or ballet. Those were the traditional standards of achievements for girls, and certain times were a real trauma for me. I graphically remember the Girl Scouts' Christmas party where the entertainment was a talent show. I didn't want to participate, but everyone nagged me until I did, threatening not to let me out of the house. Finally, I sang "In the Shoemaker's Shop" just to save myself. It was really painful, for music is not my talent. Even my children do not want to stand by me in church when we sing.

Falling in Love

BEGINNING in the fifth grade I saw boys in a different light. Where we had fought, played king of the mountain, and hated each other before, now my heart felt funny when they were around.

I loved my fifth-grade teacher Mrs. Hudson for many reasons, but one was that she read to us every day after lunch. Even though we could all read, it was so comforting to have her read to us while we rested. She read *Rebecca of Sunnybrook Farm* first and later *Kon-Tiki*. We would put our heads on our desks and listen to her sweet voice take us across the Atlantic Ocean on a raft of balsa wood.

We would sit silently with our heads resting on our crossed arms. In the early spring James Reed smiled at me from under his arm as we listened to Mrs. Hudson read. I saw him, really saw him, for the first time. His hair was dark black, and he had fair skin. He reached over and gave me a note under the desk. When I opened it, I saw, "I love you. Do you love me? Answer 'yes' or 'no'." There were two boxes, and my hand shook as I got my pencil and marked the *yes* box. I was in love.

In those days we had a devotional in the morning. The principal would pipe over the public address system a song called "Guardian Angels." At Main Street School, we also had a Bible reading and prayer every morning. "Guardian Angels" is the song I associate with James Reed. I guess I would call it our song because I can't think of it without thinking of him. We would look at each other while it played, and I thought my heart would just jump out of my chest.

On Saturday mornings the picture show in Tuscumbia would have a double or triple feature that started at 9:30. Including the "Rocket Man" serial and a cartoon, it lasted almost all day. Mother worked two doors down at the SSL department store, and I would go with her to town, wait around the store, and go on to the movie when it opened.

I would be sitting there in the dark, silent movie in one of the few double seats when James Reed would walk quietly down the carpeted aisle and slip into the seat beside me. Each week he would stop in the lobby and buy me a candy bar called "Forever Yours." He would hand it to me without a word, and nestle down in his seat. We both felt the same way without saying it.

I know that parents say that kids don't know about love, but I will never love anyone like I did James Reed in the fifth grade. We went to boy-girl parties and two-stepped to popular music in Anne Denton's basement. There was a fireplace in the middle of the room so we danced in a circle around the basement, almost not breathing. Then we would all walk around the block and back, holding hands in the warm, summer night.

Later that year James Reed took his leather belt and carved "Naomi" across the back. When he walked into the classroom that morning and I saw it, I could hardly think. My chest hurt, and I thought I would lose my breath completely or hyperventilate.

James Reed never did anything but hold my hand. His lips never so much as got close to mine, but I loved him with a passion. Maybe that's why I lost him, because later he would go on and like other girls, become known for being a good kisser, and disappear out of my life. When I hear adults make remarks about "puppy love," I know they never felt as I did about James Reed in the fifth grade. There would be many others in my life over the years, but no one ever made me feel like he did.

Children have the same feelings as adults have, maybe even more sharply. I guess Mother knew about James Reed, but she never made a comment one way or the other.

~

To fall in love, to allow ourselves to feel, to have our hearts fill up and even break, all of this comes as a part of growing up. That's important to remember, but even more important is the recognition that children have as full a range of feelings as adults: sadness, fear, disappointment, confusion, hurt, guilt, joy, excitement. Too often, we as adults assign just two feelings to children—happiness and sadness. In addition, we often downplay, discount, or even ridicule other emotions. This lack of empathy robs a child of the permission to feel all emotions, but also the permission to share all emotions.

Taking Trips at Home and Away

SINCE our house was warm and tight, my MawMaw Sanders stayed with us in the winter. We would go down to my aunt's house in Iuka when the weather began to get cool and pick up MawMaw and her things. She would stay until spring.

She had lost her home during the depression for taxes, about twenty-four dollars. After that she lived with us part of the year and Mother's sister Bama the remainder of the time. She never complained.

I know it hurt Mother when she and I went out to the Sanders homeplace a few years ago and saw that the acreage is now a big subdivision developed by a man who bought the property for the back taxes. All that I could find were a few rocks from the chimney of the homeplace.

MawMaw was born a twin, and the other twin died. She

used to tell me that as a baby she was so small that the family could fit her in a coffee pot. She was very quiet and only spoke the most important things. MawMaw usually referred to me as "Girlie." She often smelled like Vick's salve or asafetida.

After Daddy died, Mother went to work full time and did not get home until almost six o'clock. When I would come in from school in the afternoons, the only person there at first was MawMaw, sitting as close to the coal burning heater as she could get. She called that "scrooched up to the fire."

However, when I would come in, she would say, "Come here, Girlie," and at the same time reach for one of the outdated *World Books* in the nearby bookcase.

I would sit down next to her there by the fire. She wore an apron all the time even though she no longer cooked. Her straight, long hair, both dark and gray, was pulled into a ball on the back of her head.

She would take just any book and spread it out over her bony knees, the apron like a frame around the book. Picking any page, she would point to the first picture she saw and say, "What are they doing in this picture, Girlie?"

"Oh, MawMaw, that's down in Argentina on the pampas where they have those gauchos that are like cowboys."

She would turn the page and say, "What are they doing in this picture, Girlie?"

"Oh, MawMaw, that's one of those Buddhist temples in Siam, like our churches."

Flipping to the back, she would say, "Tell me about this picture."

"That's the Grand Canyon where people ride donkeys to the bottom."

We would travel all over the world in those old encyclopedias, from Japan to Iceland, from Australia to the Great Wall of China. She loved those pictures, and I loved them with her.

As a child I thought that MawMaw's eyes were old, and she could not see. As an adult I know that she could not read. The person who shared these adventures, sparked my interest in geography, and fanned my imagination could not read.

Somewhere in all of that, I see the strength and power of a parent or grandparent. They don't have to be well-educated or rich to be a big part in the life of a child. They really just have to be there and share themselves. The trips MawMaw and I took were free, but, oh, so wonderful.

The summer after seventh grade I took my first real trip. After Daddy died, Shirley learned to drive our '47 Mercury that Daddy had bought from Lang Thompson in Iuka. Pug Milligan, a friend and neighbor of our family, taught her how to drive. I sat in the back seat and listened to every word and watched every move. I actually learned to drive just by being there.

I remember that one day I was practicing my driving in the driveway and rolled out and hit a piano truck. Somehow I got the brake and the clutch confused. Mother paid the forty-five dollars to get the old Mercury repaired and life went on. We were all trying to get used to our new places and roles now that Daddy was gone.

That summer we were sitting on porch late one afternoon, and Mother said, "I think we'll go to Twilla's tomorrow." Twilla was Mother's sister who lived in south Georgia, about three hundred miles away. Mother never has believed in planning ahead for a trip since something might happen and she wouldn't be able to go. This way, she could just slip up on the trip at the last minute, and not take anything for granted.

Shirley and I took the car to the service station to be checked before the trip. We barely got there before they closed, but the man checked the tires, oil, and fan belt. We were ready.

This trip to Twilla's house was my first real trip except to Iuka. I was so excited as we packed that night to go. Shirley would drive, of course, but I knew that I would be the backup driver. At thirteen years old, I was thrilled. Because it was such a long trip, I actually got to drive a lot of the way.

When we got to Twilla's house in south Georgia, everything was new to us. She lived near the main highway that ran from New York to Miami. It was referred to as the "four-lane" and was busy with people from up North going to the beach. They drove big cars, talked funny, and had lots of money.

Twilla and her family had built a fruit stand on the highway, and it was a source of great interest to me since I had never been around anything like that. I got right in the middle of the whole business by getting in the watermelon trade. I drove our old '47 Mercury back into the truck patches, bought watermelons for five cents from local farmers, loaded them into the trunk and back seat, and took them back to the fruitstand.

We had a makeshift bench where the tourists could sit and eat watermelon under the shed of the stand, and those Northerners thought they were in the middle of Down South country life. They paid fifty cents for a slice, sat right down on those old planks, and learned to spit seeds into the grass.

To entice them in, I walked up the highway about seventy-five yards, turned an old bushel basket upside down, and placed a quarter of a watermelon on it. I printed a sign that said, "WATERMELONS $1.00." They stopped in droves to taste the fruit and sit on the side of the highway to eat it. We made a lot of money that week in Georgia and secretly laughed over how we'd taken in the tourists.

Shirley and I took turns driving back from Georgia. When

we got within a few miles of home, I saw up ahead an Alabama Highway Patrol roadblock checking drivers' licenses. I pulled over and stopped, ran around the car, and let Shirley take over.

When we rolled up to the patrolman, he looked over at me and said, "What about your license, young lady? I saw you driving."

"I don't have one," I confessed, barely meeting his eyes.

"Promise me you'll take driver's education, and I'll let you go," he offered.

"I will, I will," I said, and we drove on home from our first vacation. By this time I was a seasoned driver.

Several other times in later summers, we would be at home late in the afternoon, and my mother would say, "I think we'll go to Florida tomorrow," and we would just take off. It was truly exciting.

Later when Shirley went off to college, I was the primary driver. Actually Mother treated me like an adult in many ways, allowing me to drive, paint the house, fix screens, and work with her in the shoe department at P.N. Hirsch. However, she always protected me and made me feel like a child when I needed it.

~

A trip with a parent can be skipping stones, shooting hoops, or lying flat on the spring earth so the dandelions look like a space-age ride at Disneyland. It's the time together that really matters. Being kids together, laughing and playing games with no parent superiority, all are ways to take special trips with a child.

Learning to Work

MY mother felt it was her duty to teach me how to work. Early on, we'd work in the garden together, sticking beans and pinching worms off the cabbages. After my daddy died, I had the responsibility of cutting the yard and taking care of a lot of the chores around the house.

Mother went to work at what was then the SSL store. I think that stood for Southern Sales Liquidators out of St. Louis. SSL was a fairly inexpensive store where a customer could always get a blouse for $1.99. Most of our clothes came from there.

When I was in about the seventh grade, she decided that I needed to learn how to work with her at the store. She came home one day after work and told me she had talked with Jimmy McGregor, the manager of the store that time. She asked him if I could work with her on Saturdays. This was before we had child labor permits. He said yes, that I could work during the busy time between 10 a.m. and 2 p.m. Of course, that really put a damper on my staying all day at the picture show.

I reported at the store the next Saturday at 10 o'clock. Mother was there in her suit. All the women who worked there wore suits, and Mother had accumulated two or three. I remember that she told me that Mrs. Hendrix who worked with her had the most expensive suits. Mother said that she bought one a season, and she bought quality ones so that they would last several years. I know the message that Mother was giving me was that even if she wasn't really in a position to buy like Mrs. Hendrix, she could see the wisdom in getting work clothes like that.

The first day that I reported for work, Mother was back in the shoe department. She looked at me and said, "Now, Naomi, there are some things I want to tell you."

This was what you would call an on-the-job training session. The *first rule* she said was, "We don't jump tables here." Now, of course that didn't have any literal meaning. What she meant was, "We don't kill ourselves here." She said, "We don't jump tables, but we work steady."

That was the first rule, and she added later like a postscript, "When you're not with a customer, you're supposed to be straightening."

That meant that you were supposed to look busy whether

you were or not. It was distracting to the customers and certainly to the manager to just stand around chewing gum and not doing anything. When customers come in, tear up the merchandise, get all of the boxes open, and get the shirts tumbled and out of size, straightening the store is very important. That was what we were supposed to be doing if we didn't have a customer.

"The *second rule*," she said, "is that everybody who comes in here is the same, and we treat them right."

That laid the groundwork for the idea that there was no special treatment for customers—nobody got more or less regardless of how they looked or who they were. Mothers would bring babies with dirty diapers in for shoes, or they would come in with children and they'd be dirty and eating bananas, banana peels all over the floor, candy wrappers stuck to the sizer. We just didn't notice it. I did just what my mother always said: "You go on," and that means you do your job with kindness.

Her *third rule* was, "Give the customer what they want. Don't argue with them. If they ask for size seven, give them a size seven even though you may know that they need a nine or a ten. People want to be in charge."

In the South a small ankle and a small foot are highly prized. Many women would ask for smaller sizes, and mother would say, "If they ask for a seven, and you know they need a ten, just give them a seven. They'll work themselves up to the size they need without your help."

That was wise advice. It basically cut out the feeling that I sometimes get in a store where the clerk thinks that she is better than I am, or knows more than I do.

Later on she told me the *fourth rule:* "We don't make people buy anything."

That was the understatement of the year. Mother was never pushy, just kind and friendly, always letting the customers look at the merchandise alone. She would be there if they needed help, but she did not try to push them into buying. She had a real knack for sales.

The customer would come in and say what she wanted or just say she was looking. If she said she was looking, Mother backed right off and went back to some little job. In the process of walking off she would say "Well, call me if you need me."

If the customer said, "I'm looking for Sunday shoes, or a pair of white heels," Mother would show them what she had in their size.

They would sit in the chair, and she would place the shoes beside them, saying, "You try them on and see if you need another size." She believed people like to try on their own shoes.

She would go off and keep working. She did not sit there

and watch every move a customer made. Her method took a lot of pressure off the customer. I watched this little way that she handled people, and it was respectful but it was also effective in sales.

And so we started to work together. I really enjoyed working with Mother. More importantly, I learned so much about people, how to talk to them, and how to work with the other people in the store.

I remember another woman, several years younger than Mother. I had the impression that Mother was the most respected employee, and this woman was envious of her place. She would try to get to a customer before Mother did. There has always been an understanding that salespeople take turnabout if they are all selling the same thing. You try to show a lot of respect because these are people you work with every day. In the end that woman left and Mother stayed on.

Working with those people and learning that ritual of respect in the store was a big part of my learning to work. Over the long haul, just getting ahead and making a sale was not the important thing. Mother made that very plain.

When I was about fourteen, I worked all day on Saturday as an extra and so did my sister Shirley, who was in college. We handled our money differently. Shirley would work Friday nights and Saturday. She would collect the clothes she wanted and put them on layaway at the store. Then she would work and pay them off. I usually borrowed my clothes from her because I was not nearly as responsible with my money. I went out with my friends and spent my whole day's earnings.

It is interesting that, after I worked all day for five dollars, Mother never interfered with how I spent the money. She knew it was the work itself that had value, and if I wanted to work hard all day and blow the money, that would be a hard lesson for me to learn, but a necessary one.

At Christmas one year I took all my knowledge and branched out, crossing the street to work at Sherman's. In addition to selling, I was given the job as wrapper when I wasn't busy. People would come in, buy twelve or fifteen pairs of ladies panties and ask me to wrap them all individually. I did it, like Mother had taught me, because that was my job.

Sometimes the manager would send me over to the Sherman's store in Florence, but I didn't like that nearly as much. When I worked at the Tuscumbia Sherman's, Mother and I would go to lunch together or bring our lunch together as we had done when I had worked with her. There was a restaurant in Tuscumbia called the V-Grill, and once in awhile we would go there, but mother thought that sixty cents for lunch was high. I know she was right because sixty cents out of a five- or six-dollar day *was* too much.

I worked at Sherman's for awhile and then moved to the Grand Leader, a store in Tuscumbia owned by one of maybe the only two or three Jewish families in town. It was a department store exactly like SSL but with a little better quality merchandise. The people working there were so different. Without the protection of my mother, I was in the middle all the time of what we would call a "cat fight" among the clerks, most of whom were middle-aged women.

I worked at the Grand Leader for two years, and certain customers stick in my memory. One Saturday, an old farmer in overalls came in and asked me for a bracer. I had no idea what he meant, but I didn't want to act dumb. I thought I would fish around and said, "What size do you need?"

He said, "A 42D."

With that I knew he wanted what we called then a brassiere. *Bra* was not a word we used in the fifties. I began to pull out those big cotton brassieres, and he would hold each one up and look at it, saying, "No, not big enough."

Finally, I got down under the table where the really big sizes were and got up to the 50, 52, 54 and finally up to the 56. Now the 56 had enough material in it for a bed sheet. It had huge cups. That old farmer held up that 56D as high as he could, and the end of it still just about touched the floor.

Running his hand and fist around the inside the cup, he said with satisfaction, "Yeah, that's her. I'll take it."

My only regret about working there happened one Saturday when an old man came in drunk with his Social Security check. It was the first week of the month, and he wanted to buy a new "suit of clothes." Over the next hour he spent almost all of his Social Security check. He bought shoes, underwear, a shirt and tie, a suit, and a hat.

For a long time afterwards, I worried that I had been a part of taking money that maybe his family needed or he owed for medical bills or that he would not have food that month. It worried me. I also wondered if he would have bought so much if he had been sober. The amount was well over a hundred dollars and, in 1955, that was a lot of money. After he left and I had rung up the sale with my number on the ticket, all the other salespeople were envious of my big sale, but it never felt good to me.

During college I applied at a shoe store in Sheffield, which is the town between Tuscumbia and Florence. The manager interviewed me and hired me as an extra. He told me that instead of working for a salary, I would get a straight seven percent commission. I wasn't sure what that meant, but I agreed and showed up the next Saturday to work.

One of the most embarrassing events of my life took place that first morning. It was a pretty high class shoe store where they had brands like Life Stride and Red Cross. When I showed up there in my SSL flats that I had worn for quite a while, the manager looked at my feet and said, "You can't work here wearing those shoes. You'll have to buy some."

He sold me a pair of flats for $10.99. I was thinking that was two weeks' salary, but, as a young person in that situation, I didn't think I had any choice but to buy a pair of bone flats with a little bow on the toe.

The first day, I sold three hundred dollars worth of shoes. I couldn't tell if the manager was mad or glad as he paid me the twenty-one dollars, minus the cost of my new shoes. I ended up with more than I had ever made on a Saturday.

I worked on commission for another couple or three weeks and then he said, "I can't afford that much."

The next week he cut me back to five percent. The first few weeks I worked were in the spring around Easter, and after that I really had to hustle to sell enough to equal what I had been making at SSL and the Grand Leader.

From that experience I learned a lot about how easy it is to be taken advantage of in the workplace. I also learned how to work a completely different group of people who came into the store. The people who came into the shoe store were people with "money".

Those years working retail were an education in how to treat people, how to push yourself when you don't feel like it, how to give back, and how to give a good day's work. I also earned ready money to go out with my friends and have a good time, and I learned very quickly to see the value of my own money.

But out of all these memories, the experience that stands out most was that my mother taught me how to work. She taught me the very basic principles of responsibility, yet that word was never used or discussed.

~

One of the things that we often hear among parents is that children don't know anything about responsibility. But I have come to see that responsibility, learning how to work, and being dependable are not inherent or innate characteristics. We must, indeed, learn these important values. The very best way to teach them is through example, working together, demonstrating those work habits, and reinforcing them in our children. Mother was right. She needed to teach me how to work.

Mother worked retail until she was almost eighty. She loved

it so much. When she was in her late eighties, I took her up to Davis', the last place she worked, and she said, "You know, I would have worked free. I still love being around the merchandise."

Going Home

GOING home is a slowing down, a settling, a time of remembering. I usually drive in silence, looking to see how high the cotton has grown, wondering who has moved into the numerous rental houses along the highway, and noticing the new colored windows in the small country churches. Sometimes on Sunday I see the church at Wheeler let out late, and I see dressed-up, laughing families stand and talk in groups out front. They are in no hurry at all to leave, and their children play in the red clay around the cars.

This weekly trip alone takes me back, moves me into another place in time, and changes my sense of myself. As I drive these miles, I am returning home, not to a place but to a feeling. If we can indeed regain our sense of total protection, warmth, and timelessness, it must be in the act of going home.

Seeing the first sign announcing Tuscumbia, Alabama, I am filled with a different sensation. It is a return to childhood, to being cared for, to the acceptance of dependence in the only setting where it is acceptable. Nowhere else have I ever allowed myself to truly depend on or count on another person.

Driving through the old part of town where oaks and elms meet over the street, I remember those childhood days of great success and heartbreaking failure. Nowhere else are those feelings of innocence and hurt so tightly intertwined.

Down that familiar street . . . I think first of walking home from school with childhood friends and later with a special boy who bought me a silver medallion necklace at Christmas. He appeared unexpectedly at my door, presented it with a blush and without a word, and hurried back to the car where his mother waited.

Down that familiar street . . . They came to my Girl Scout Troop meeting that spring day. We met at the old community center that had been a train depot in past years, and they drove me down that street to my house where I would hear that my father had died that day, killed on the job ten miles away. I wore my mint green organdy Easter dress with its black velvet belt to the funeral. Louise Wells, the neighbor across the street washed and ironed it. Later, she would be the one who prepared the reception after my wedding.

Down that familiar street . . . In the five blocks from Main Street to my home, the houses decline in value the further I go from town and the nearer I get to the railroad tracks. We lived in the "West End" of town, and it was just not as acceptable as the "East End."

Down that familiar street . . . Hurrying home late at night from friends, driving the old '55 too fast, I hoped to get there early enough not to arouse disapproval and suspicion. The quarter's worth of gas we all chipped in to buy at the Savings Station was gone, and I was coasting home like a rabbit to his hole, safe.

Each time I drive that street those memories fold around me, and I return home—not to a place, but to a feeling. Even now when I run up the steps to my home place and go in, I smell *home*. I realized long ago that every family has a distinct smell. It's not good or bad, just different.

That familiar smell rises up as I hit the front door, and sends me reeling back my childhood. Mother did not wear perfume when I was a child. She smelled like Mother. There is no other way to describe it. It was a mixture of clean and warm. In the house, the mingling of coal burning, furniture polish, and green beans cooking all melted together somehow to make our distinct family smell. No one else's house ever smelled like ours, and it still smells that way to me.

In my early years, home was hearing Mother and Daddy talk in bed late at night and early in the morning. Lying in bed nearby, I would hear them in the kitchen before daylight, their voices full of love and affection. The tone of his voice was different, softer and gentler, when he talked to her. In the hours before daylight the sounds of their time together were laced with the smell of biscuits and bacon.

Today when I step into that living room, I see the beveled mirror over the mantel that almost shattered the day I threw a green peach at my sister. Shirley wanted me to make cornbread before Mother got home from her job, but I resisted every day. I see the hearth where my father's casket sat. The den sofa sits now where the old coal-burning stove warmed me and my grandmother after school each day. Sometimes I can still see Aunt Josie there visiting my MawMaw and whispering about old times. MawMaw would say nothing. She seldom did.

Driving down that street and going in that house, I know without a doubt what home really is. It is never bought and sold at the store. It is never pictured in a catalog or described in an advertisement. It is truly where hearts and souls tenderly touch each other with a kiss, a hug, a word of encouragement. It has nothing to do with brick and mortar, square feet, or the number of fireplaces. Home is the feeling of being safe and loved and where all you have to do to earn this is to "show up."

About the Author

Naomi Haines Griffith grew up in Alabama, Mississippi, and Tennessee. She earned a B.S. from the University of North Alabama, an M.A. from the George Peabody College at Vanderbilt University, and a Masters in Social Work from the University of Alabama. She worked in child welfare systems from 1966 until 1984, when she became Executive Director of PACT, a pioneer child abuse prevention agency she helped to found.

Since 1988, Naomi Griffith has become a national speaker and consultant on child welfare issues. A well-known storyteller and family issues specialist, she uses humor and her own experiences to challenge and inspire her audiences.